For mothers of toddlers
  and mothers of teens
And mothers of all the
  in-betweens,
For mothers-to-be
  with wonder filled,
And grandmothers, too,
  so proud and thrilled,
For mothers of daughters
  all sugar and spice,
And mothers of sons
  (who are equally nice),
For aunts and cousins,
  whoever they are,
And friends and relatives
  near and far,
For all who have known
  to their hearts' content
The love of a child—
  this book is meant.

# Chin up, mom

VERSES BY
SUZANNE DOUGLASS

ILLUSTRATED BY
ROLAND RODEGAST

Published by The C.R. Gibson Company
Norwalk, Connecticut

CONTENTS

# THE PREGNANT PERIOD

## TIP-OFF

How do I know that I'm pregnant?
A very simple way.
I'm living on soda crackers
And gaining a pound a day.

## THE WOES OF
## A LADY IN WAITING

The butcher, the baker,
The candle-stick maker,
All hail me with jocular greeting.
Friends and relations
Surpress exclamations
And show their surprise at each meeting.

Folks call up at dawn
To find out if I've gone;
It's trying enough to be late.
Next time the stork's due,
They can beg till they're blue,
But I'm darned if I'll forecast the date.

## JUST AROUND THE CORNER

Shopping for my first layette,
I go from store to store.
But shopping now is different
Than it ever was before.

By the time I've bought the booties
And the little sacques and gown,
I'll know where every rest-room is
In every store in town.

## ENLARGEMENT UPON A THEME

My shirttail's out,
   My skirt's unzipped,
      Life has a new dimension:
I've grown to see
   Maternity
      As the mother of extension.

## A ROSE BY ANY NAME

Should you call her Mary Ann,
Your precious baby girl;
Martha, Joyce or Evelyn,
Linda, Jane or Pearl?

Elizabeth or Pamela,
Kathleen, Elaine, Simone?
It makes no difference which you choose;
She'll hate it when she's grown.

## A WORD TO THE NEWLY MARRIED

Enjoy your meals by yellow candlelight
On linen table cloths, unstained and white
With dinner conversation gay and bright
Centered around the latest book or play;
Oh, yes, enjoy it fully while you may ...

Because, when families grow, the change is drastic,
The cloths give way to place-mats made of plastic,
The conversation grows much less elastic ...

And believe it or not, there'll come a day
You'll find yourself entreating,
"Please, dear, don't put the puppy on the table
While we're eating."

IT   DIDN'T
COME FROM HIGH-
HEELED  SHOES,  THIS
POSTURE THAT YOU SEE;
ALTHOUGH MY SPINE'S
NOT ON A LINE
THE  FAULT
RESTS NOT
WITH ME.
IT WAS
CAUSED
BACK IN
MY  TEENAGE
BY  THE  BOOKS
I HAD  TO  CARRY
AND  I  THOUGHT IT
WOULD   CORRECT  IT-
SELF  WHEN  I  LEFT
SCHOOL  TO  MARRY.
BUT  NOW  THAT  I'M
A  MATRON  THERE'S
AN EVEN GREATER
DIP;  I  SIMPLY
TRADED TEXT
BOOKS FOR
A BABY ON
MY  HIP.

# EARLY MOTHERHOOD

### DAWN PATROL

The clock on the dresser says 4 a.m.
The house is dark and still.
I tiptoe into the baby's room
And stand by his crib until
He stirs from his froggy position,
His bottom up in the air,
Then I rearrange his blankets
To cover the spots that are bare
And go back, reassured, to my bedroom
As darkness begins to soften;
I knew all along he was breathing,
I just had to check on how often.

### BABY'S KISS

There's nothing like a
   baby's kiss,
Nothing experienced yet.
Nothing's as gentle,
Nothing's as sweet—
And nothing is half as wet.

## ROCKABY BABY

He's fussy whenever I pick him up,
   He screams when I ignore him.
He really doesn't know what he wants
   But he'll cry till I get it for him.

## THE LIFE
## OF THE PARTY

The hostess' mother is overworked;
The hostess is cross and sleepy.
She missed her nap and so did the guests
And they're all inclined to be
   weepy.

Half of the kids are too young
   for the games
And the other half are too old.
And one little boy won't give
   up his gift
No matter how often he's told.

And though every child wants a
   frosting rose,
The hostess won't spoil the bouquet,
So the cake's finally cut amid
   sniffles and tears,
Which leaves just one thing left
   to say—
      HAPPY BIRTHDAY.

## THE SECRET OF
## PHYSICAL FITNESS

Some folks go for skiing.
Others chase pop flies.
But I pursue a wire cart
Loaded with supplies.

Some folks swing at golf balls.
Other folks skip rope.
But I play catch with oranges
And juggle bars of soap.

Many folks spend money
Keeping fit and strong ...
I just go supermarketing
And take the kids along.

## MORE IF'S THAN ARF'S

If you can keep on smiling
And looking at your best
With dog hair on your trousers
And paw prints on your chest;

If you don't object to rising
At the faintest crack of dawn
And strolling outdoors in the rain
With just your bathrobe on;

If you can keep your temper
And discount with a shrug
Puddles in the hallway
And stains upon the rug;

If you can calm a neighbor
Whose garden's been dug up,
Then you're the kind of parent
Whose child should have a pup.

## ADVICE FROM THE MANAGER

If you get in a fight,
Bite.
If you get bit back,
Hit back.
Then, if you still aren't
    winning the battle,
Tattle.

## IN THE STILL OF THE NIGHT

What a saintly picture she presents,
That silhouette in the chair,
Soothing the fretful infant
With tender, loving care.
It's a picture that shows devotion
And patience in every line ...
A mother and her baby ...
It's simple in design.
But there's a deeper meaning here
That's hid from the beholder;
The hand that rocks the cradle *aches*
Clear up to the shoulder.

## EXCHANGE PROGRAM

The children cleaned out their toybox today,
But they wouldn't throw one single old toy away.
Still the project was rescued from utter defeat—
They returned what belonged to the kids down the street,
An improvement I'd view with great relief,
Except, I'm afraid that it's doomed to be brief—
Tomorrow the other kids' mothers will fuss
And make them bring back what belongs to us.

## NO SKIPPING ALOUD

They've outgrown bedtime stories,
No matter what their ages,
As soon as they become aware
That you are skipping pages.

## CHILD'S WORLD AT ARM'S LENGTH

I've learned about a child's world
   From holding little boys
In front of candy counters
   And before displays of toys;
From lifting them to windows
   To look at distant places;
From boosting them to mirrors
   To prove dirt's on their faces;
From holding them above the crowds
   To watch paraders revel,
I've learned about a child's world:
   It's all below see level.

## HIS AND HERS

There is a little girl
And she has a little curl
Right in the middle of her forehead,
And when she is good
She is Daddy's little girl;
She's Mommy's little girl when she's
     horrid.

## TODDLERS

Once they begin
To toddle about,
They're never tucked in
Until you're tuckered out.

## TOYLAND

His little toy dog is covered with dust,
And so are his little toy blocks.
I bought them and paid an extravagant price,
So what does he play with? The box.

## TURNING THE TABLES

Babies get most of their food on their faces,
Their hair, their ears, and similar places;
And we adults are always berating them,
When instead, we ought to be imitating them ...
And then, although we'd be messy at dinner,
At least, we'd be a whole lot thinner.

## FROM OUT OF THE PAST

Breathes there a mother who doesn't feel old,
With a bottle to warm and the diapers to fold,
Watching a movie on TV—late,
That she saw at a drive-in once,
        on a date.

## HALF SAFE

Careless children lose their gloves.
This never happens to my son.
For he's a very careful child ...
He never loses more than one.

## SO MUCH, SO SOON

No one minds a little pitcher
Having big ears
Until he starts to understand
What he overhears.

## POSITIVE THINKING

I'm mad about injections
  And beg for penicillin.
I'm cheerful in the dentist's chair
  Especially when he's drillin'.

I lick my lips for castor oil,
  Think vitamins are dandy,
Enjoy the sting of iodine,
  Eat vegetables like candy.

But I'm no hypochondriac,
  Although the signs are ample;
I'm just a mother, martyred
  To set a good example.

## DAYS OF
## WHINE AND REASONS

When children nag for some expensive toy,
I've learned the only way to peace and quiet
Is to prove to them that they don't really want it.
The way I do that is—go out and buy it!

## THE MUD PACK

No matter how much I scrub and comb,
No matter what high hopes I start the day with,
My kids always look like the kind of kids
I wouldn't want my kids to play with.

## THE FAMILY DINES OUT

I finished my meal relaxed and calm,
A feeling new to me, and strange;
For the worst behaved kids at the restaurant
Were somebody else's—for a change.

## THE DEEP END

No normal child who thrives on mud'll
    Ever walk around a puddle.

## WATER, WATER EVERYWHERE

A child can bathe from head to toe
And get himself clean in an hour or so,
Which is roughly half the time it takes
His mother to clean up the mess he makes.

## DENTAL DEDUCTIONS

If the tube is squ-u-ushed,
    The kids have brushed.

## PONY RIDES

Round and round and round they go—
Around the circle trail;
The children on the ponies,
The parents on the rail.

Three rides for a quarter
And any little laddie
Can blow two dollars at the track
Quicker than his daddy.

```
┌─────────────────────────┐
│              THE        │
│            P T A        │
│          PERIOD         │
└─────────────────────────┘
```

## ARTISTIC APPRECIATION

That yellow circle is the sun.
That oblong shape below
With windows in it, is a house.
Those spots are flakes of snow.
That red thing is a chimney,
And that wavy line is smoke.
And that purple dot is nothing,
It's just where the crayon broke.
The black line is the sidewalk.
Those green streaks are the grass;
And it's hanging on the blackboard
In front of all the class!
My daughter's name is on it,
Artistically misspelt;
It's beautiful ... and now I know
How Rembrandt's mother felt.

## MISFORTUNE'S CHILD

His parents are happy together.
There is no talk of divorce.
His father neither drinks nor bets
His pay check on a horse.

He knows neither riches nor poverty.
He lives in a nice neighborhood.
By his family he's loved and wanted.
By his teachers he's understood.

He has brothers and sisters to play with.
Poor kid, what a lousy break.
With his happy youth, he'll have nothing to blame
For a single adult mistake.

## SMALL WORLD

As long as I have my hair combed
And I'm well groomed, head to toe,
I could stand all day at the corner of Main
And not see a soul that I know.
But if I'm unkempt and bedraggled
Like a cat that got caught in the rain,
I'd run smack into the minister's wife
On the Serengeti Plain.

## DOWN MEMORY LANE

The oldest words of pen or tongue:
We didn't do that when I was young.

## ACCIDENTS WILL HAPPEN

The clock got knocked off the mantle.
The screen got torn in the door.
The china's chipped, the mirror's cracked,
And the tile is loose on the floor.
A ball came through the window
In this morning's baseball game—
If my kids come from a broken home,
They have only themselves to blame.

## LONG DISTANCE
## or
## SADDEST STORY EVER TOLLED

If you call her person to person,
Your wife is at home alone;
If you dial direct, she ran next door
And your three-year-old answers the phone.

## A CLASS BY HERSELF

Breathes there a woman who's never wept
Tears of joy with the coming of Sept.?
If so, I'll bet this remarkable creature
Isn't a mother; she's a teacher.

## REVELATIONS

No family hides its secrets well
Whose children shine at *show and tell*.

### TEMPORARY CRAMNESIA

At night the children watch TV
Sprawled round the set in a semi-circle.
What oversight will suddenly be
    remembered at bedtime?
Their homework'll.

### THE SILENT TREATMENT

Forgive me if I don't applaud and cheer—
The Christmas play was splendid!
My son didn't have a line to speak,
But I'm not in the least offended
That he wasn't given an angel's part
Or chosen to sing in the choir;
To see him onstage as a shepherd or sage
Was never my heart's desire.
Please understand, it's not sour grapes.
I really don't care two thumps
That my son was cast as the camel—
I'm just beat from stuffing his humps!

### THEATRICAL REVIEW

I've seen a good school play
    at last;
Just one.
You'll never guess who's in
    the cast ...
My son!

## MOTHER, CAN YOU SPARE A MINUTE?

Oh, please, DO BE on the refreshment
   committee;
It won't take much time, and your cakes
   are so pretty.
And DO BE in charge of the membership
   drive;
The first meeting's Thursday, three-
   thirty to five.
Did you know we're getting new playground
   equipment?
DO BE there to help us unpack the first
   shipment.
And DO BE on hand the first Friday in May
To dress the first grade for the Mother's
   Day play.
Which sums up my life as a P.T.A. mother—
One DO-BE-ous honor on top of another.


## DRAMA BEHIND THE SCENES

She made her debut in the Halloween play
As a witch in *The Dance of the Brooms.*
In the Valentine play, she had nothing to say
But she wore a heart headdress with plumes.
As a tulip in May, she wore paper-mache
And sang in a chorus of "blooms."
For the ten minute total she was on display,
I spent all year making costumes.

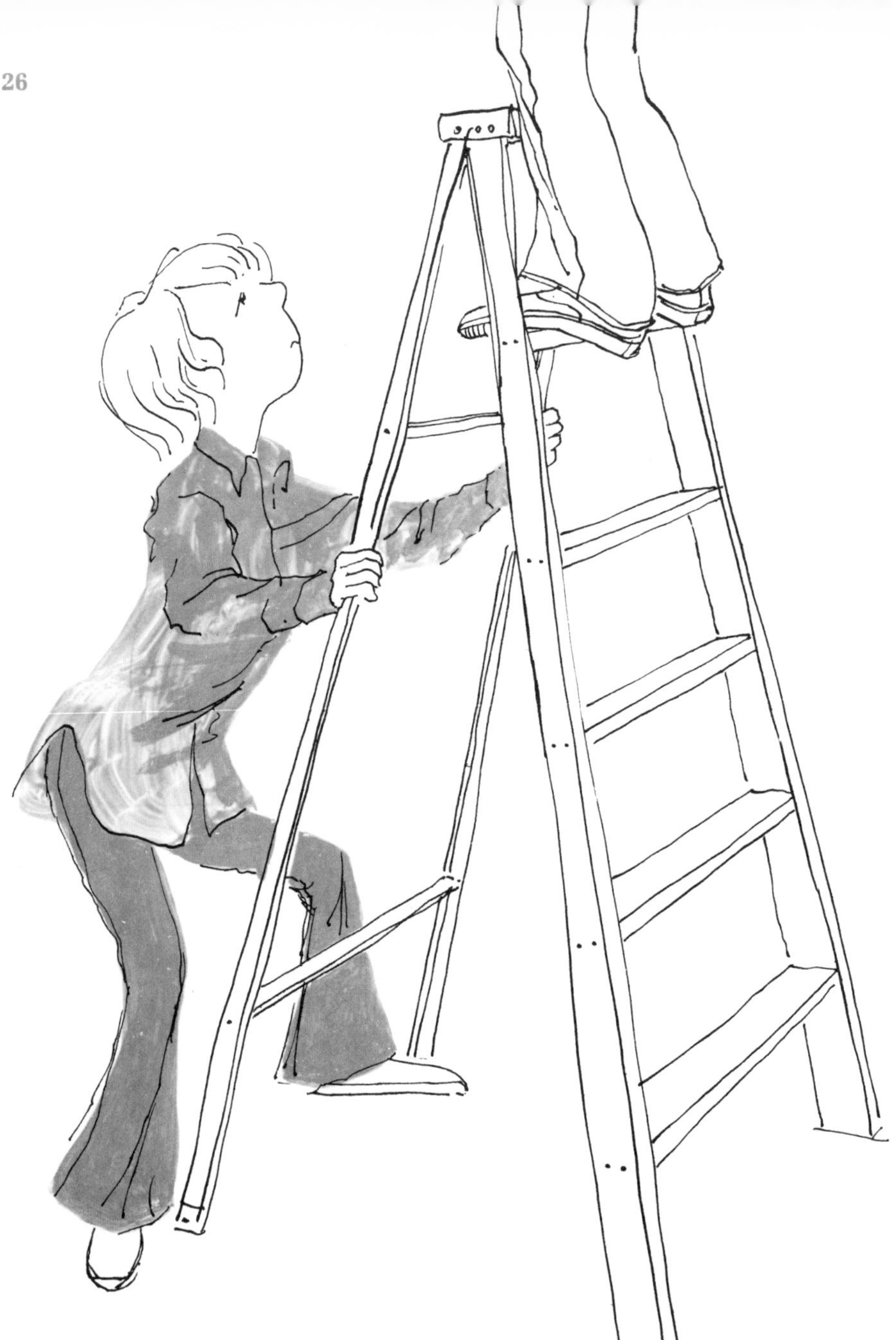

# REFLECTIONS ON FAMILY LIFE

## WITH A SLIGHT ASSIST

We measure the square feet,
Sketch the designs,
Balance the levels,
Chalk the chalk lines.

We stir up the paint,
Hold boards while they saw,
Hold nails while they hammer,
Sand out every flaw.

We clean sticky brushes,
Untangle kinked wires,
Mix canfuls of glue,
Hand them the pliers.

We steady their ladders,
Fetch tools from the shelves;
We're the wives of the husbands
Who "do it themselves."

## FLY-BY-NIGHT

No wonder dear old Santa Claus
Is such a jolly soul—
By the first of the month
When the bills come in,
He's safely back at the Pole.

## NO KIDDING

There's just one thing
About sibling rivalry:
It's very rough on
Parent's survivalry.

## YOU CAN'T GET THERE FROM HERE—
## ANY FASTER THAN I'M GOING

It's thirty-five miles to grandma's
From the turnoff at State Road
   Nine,
It's twenty-five miles from the
   railroad track,
Ten miles from the county line.

I've learned the distance from
   town to town,
Billboard to billboard ... cow to
   cow ...
In response to a back-seat chorus:
"Mother, how far is it now?"

## TWO BRIEF MOMENTS

We've reached that tranquil period
When we can breathe with ease;
Our daughter is mid-way between
Diapers and dungarees.

Our son has also reached that plain
Toward which all parents strive—
Old enough to wash his neck
But still too young to drive.

## FACE TO PHASE

Little girls are want and wiggle;
Teenage girls are gab and giggle.

Little boys are raggle-tag.
Teenage boys are boast and brag.

And parents who are wits and sages
More easily survive both stages.

## THE SCUFFED OXFORD STOMP

Downtrodden by your
    offspring?
If your reply is "nay,"
You've never had the aisle
    seat
At a children's matinee.

## TRUTH AND CONSEQUENCES

It isn't difficult at all
To keep up with the Joneses.
The trouble comes in keeping up
The payments on your loanses.

## BEST LAID PLANS

Plan a picnic at the lake;
Fry a chicken, bake a cake.

Plan a weekend motor trip;
Have the car checked, pack a grip.

Plan a visit out of state;
Make arrangements, choose a date.

Then, whatever day you pick,
That's the day the kids get sick!

## LONG-RANGE WEATHER PREDICTION

WINTER

Unseasonably sunny weather ahead.
(Santa brought the kids a sled).

SPRING

Freak snowstorm the following day
After you pack the quilts away.

SUMMER

Cloudy with rain all over the nation
From stem to stern of your vacation.

FALL

Wind in gusts of near-gale force—
After you've raked the leaves, of course.


## HUSH, CHILD

I thought when Johnny learned to read
I'd be so pleased and proud;
I didn't know when John learned
To read ... he'd read *out loud*.

## MOTHER'S DICTIONARY
## OF FOODS

Meat ...
    Just two kinds are eaten
    From toddlers to teeners;
    One is hamburger ...
    The other is wieners.

Potatoes ...
    The star of the platter,
    They're known far and wide.
    All children love them—
    But only fried.

Vegetables ...
    To do you a favor,
    A youngster may take
    A spoonful of these
    If you bribe him with cake.

Milk ...
    A bland tasting liquid
    To wash down the food
    That kids swallow whole—
    Untasted, unchewed.

Bread ...
    The true staff of life,
    Makes kids strong and robust.
    To avoid tearful scenes
    You can trim off the crust.

Cake ...
  After pleading to get it,
  A typical kid'll
  Eat off the frosting
  And crumble the middle.


## TO EACH HIS OWN

In past years we taught him to share his toys
And candy with neighborhood girls and boys
Unselfishly. And our teaching paid.
Now often his teenage friends invade
Our kitchen bent on an icebox raid—
A development which, if we'd only known,
We'd have certainly let well enough alone.


## HEAD START

The advantage of startin'
Kids in kindergarten
Before they begin public schools
Is not so they'll learn
How to make a clay urn
Or construct a toy wagon from spools ...

It's the two extra terms
To expose them to germs
That profits them most, I'm afraid;
For with fair luck, by June,
They're completely immune
And won't lose any time in first grade.

## BY AN IRONING BOARD

I think that I shall never cease
   To wonder as I sprinkle,
Why cloth that will not hold a crease
   Holds every wrinkle.

## LINES TO A WIFE OVER A MENU

I'm ordering strawberry shortcake
So I warn you before it's too late.
If you don't want dessert, that's
   all right, dear,
*But keep your fork out of my plate.*

## IF

If you have a lion's courage
And a very thick skin,
If you're blessed with friendly neighbors
And sympathetic kin,
If you're a super-salesman
And not an easy quitter,
Perhaps you'll find a home for
Every kitten in the litter.

## INTERIOR DECORATION

Some homes are furnished with pastel chairs
And antique bric-a-brac
And thick white rugs from wall to wall
Across the floor and back.

And some homes have expensive lamps
And glass topped tables, nested,
And potted plants in wrought iron stands
All growing unmolested ...

And candy dishes sitting 'round
With rosebuds on their little lids,
And full length mirrors on the walls—
And other homes have little kids.

## GRANDMOTHER

She lets him go barefoot in
    summertime
And swing on the garden gate.
She lets him eat cookies
    between his meals
And stay up disgracefully late.

She indulges him when he visits;
She was stricter with her boy.
But this one isn't hers to
    raise—
Only to enjoy.

## PARTY GIRL

Today the key to social success
Has nothing to do with brains or wit;
It isn't what you know, but who ...
And if she's free to baby sit.

## INSIDE STORY

When the home is where the heart is,
The parlor is where the grade-school art is.

## EGGS-ACTLY

As I stand here coloring Easter eggs
In every conceivable hue
From pink that borders on purple
To green that borders on blue,
I think of the children's faces
And how they'll light with pleasure
To see the eggs the bunny has brought
And a basket for good measure.

As I stand here coloring Easter eggs
I'm only human, I guess;
I think of tomorrow, eggshells on the floor,
And I'll have to clean up the mess:
And the meals I'll prepare using hard-boiled eggs—
I'll pickle 'em, devil 'em, slaw 'em;
But most of all, I think of the hen
And how she'd react if she saw 'em!

## ABOUT FACE (RED)

The parent-child relationship
With passing time grows grim;
By the time he stops embarrassing
    you,
You'll start embarrassing him.

## POINT OF VIEW

The happiness within a home
Depends more frequently
On things that mothers overlook
Than things they oversee.

## THANKSGIVING RESOLUTION

Next time the roast is overdone,
The car won't start, the mail is late,
The baby sitter doesn't come,
My spouse forgets our wedding date ...

Next time the puppy wets the floor,
Unexpected guests appear,
The phone rings when I'm in the tub,
My bossy in-laws interfere ...

Next time it clouds and looks like rain
When I've just hung the washing out,
I'll fuss and fume—and thank the Lord
That's all I have to complain about.

## ARISE, MY LOVE

The toast is burnt; the coffee's weak—
It's amber in the cup.
There's no hot water, either;
The children used it up.

The clock stopped and I overslept
(I'm wakeful as a rule).
I'll have to write the kids a note;
They'll all be late for school.

The morning paper's on the roof;
That newsboy's such a clown.
You'll have to get a ladder
If you want to get it down.

The car won't start. I tried it
But I think the battery's dead.
Arise, my love, and greet the dawn ...
I'm going back to bed.

## MONKEY SEE, MONKEY DO

Children mimic grown-ups;
They ape us to the letter
No matter how much time we take
To try to teach them better.

## LIFE'S GARDEN

Mother is the blossom ...
Radiant, complete.
The children are the tiny buds ...
Delicate and sweet.
Father is the sturdy stem
That holds them straight and tall.
Love is the root that gives them life
And nourishes them all.


## REVOLTING DEVELOPMENT

From raking the leaves to mowing the lawn
To setting the dinner table,
Most children like to be helpful—
Till they're old enough to be able.


## TURNABOUT

Worse than being wakened up
By a neighbor's howling pup
Is worrying for fear your pup
Is gonna wake the neighbors up.

# ACKNOWLEDGMENTS

*Thanks are due to the following publications
for permission to reprint the material indicated:*

THE AMERICAN LEGION MAGAZINE: "Proper Outlook."

EXPECTING: "By Any Name"; "Woes of a Lady in Waiting."

FAMILY WEEKLY: "About Face"; "Baby's Kiss"; "Best-laid Plans";
"Eggs-actly"; "Family Dines Out"; "From Out of the Past"; "Head
Start"; "More If's Than Arf's"; "Party Girl"; "Revolting
Development"; "Temporary Cramnesia"; "To Each His Own"; "With
A Slight Assist."

FARM JOURNAL: "Truth and Consequences."

GIRL TALK: "In the Still of the Night."

GOOD HOUSEKEEPING: "Advice From The Manager"; "Deep End";
"Half Safe"; "His and Hers"; "If"; "Long Range Weather Forecast";
"Mother's Dictionary of Foods"; "Water, Water Everywhere."

LADIES' HOME JOURNAL: "Artistic Appreciation"; "Dawn Patrol";
"Down Memory Lane"; "Grandma"; "In A Class by Herself"; "Life
of the Party"; "No Kidding"; "Positive Thinking"; "Rockabye Baby";
"You Can't Get There From Here."

LOOK: "Dental Deductions."

MC CALL'S: "Accidents Will Happen"; "Days of Whine and Reasons";
"Drama Behind the Scenes"; "Exchange Program"; "Fly by Night";
"Inside Story"; "No Skipping Aloud"; "Secret of Physical Fitness";
"Silent Treatment."

SATURDAY EVENING POST: "Arise, My Love"; "By an Ironing Board";
"Child's World at Arm's Length"; "Lines to a Wife Over a Menu";
"Mud Pack"; "Mother, Can You Spare A Minute?"; "Pony Rides";
"The Scuffed Oxford Stomp"; "Small World"; "Theatrical Review";
"Word to the Newly Married."

SECRETS: "Interior Decoration"; "Thanksgiving Resolution."

WALL STREET JOURNAL: "Hush, Child"; "Long Distance"; "Misfortune's
Child"; "Monkey See, Monkey Do"; "So Much, So Soon"; "Turnabout";
"Two Brief Moments."